Play the Harmonica TODAY!

A Revolutionary Technique for Learning to Play the Blues, Rock, & Folk Harmonica

David Harp

Mud Puddle Books
NEW YORK

A Few Other Books by David Harp:

• Instant Blues Harmonica (Volumes I and II) • Instant Chromatic Harmonica • Instant Guitar • Instant Flute • The Instant Harmonica Kit for Kids • Harmonica Positions • The Three Minute Meditator • Me and My Harmonica • Instant Blues/Rock Harmonica: The Video • Make Me Musical: Instant Harmonica • Metaphysical Fitness • The Three Minute Meditator Audiotape • How To Whistle Like A Pro • Bending the Blues • EarthCards • The New Three Minute Meditator • The Instant Rhythm Kit • How To Save Your Back, Neck, and Shoulders In Ten Minutes A Day • Country & Western Harmonica Made Easy • Music Theory Made Easy • Instant Harmonica for Kids (Video) • The Pocket Harmonica Songbook • Three Minutes to™ Blues Harmonica (Video) • Blues & Rock Harmonica Made Easy • How to Fight a Cold and Win • And more coming!

Play the Harmonica—Today!
A Revolutionary Technique for Learning to Play the Blues, Rock, & Folk Harmonica
by David Harp

Originally published as
Three Minutes to Blues, Rock, & Folk Harmonica!
by Musical I. Press

© 1998 Musical I. Press

This edition published in 2005 by
Mud Puddle Books, Inc.
54 W. 21st Street
Suite 601
New York, NY 10010

info@mudpuddlebooks.com

ISBN: 1-59412-099-4

Printed and bound in China

Contents

Play the Blues—Today! • 25

Play Rock and Roll—Today! • 36

Play Folk Music—Today! • 42

Introduction ❶

Hi! I'm David Harp. I've been creating harmonica instruction for more than 20 years. And I think that this "**Harmonica Style Sampler**" just might be my best beginner's method, ever! Why? Because it's the simplest. It will get you ready to play almost any style of music right away. Hard to believe? Try me — it's true! After less than ten minutes of hands-on, mouth-on basics, you'll be ready to start playing your own Blues, Rock, or Folk songs!

The Book and the CD:
Learn by Eye, Learn by Ear

I created this method as a book and CD package, although each part (book and CD) can be used separately.

Some things in the book (like the "Boogie Woogie Playalongs," or the "Chicago Twelve Bar Blues," for instance) work best when played along with good background music. And there's plenty of that on the CD, of course.

Many other parts — like the Folk Songs, the "Bluesy Train," the "Solo Blues" and "Solo Rock" songs, and the "Solo Boogie" — are meant to be played without any background music.

Some of us learn better from reading, and some of us learn better from listening — it's up to you! Why not try both?

I'll put in a little number in a circle, like the **1** on the preceding page, to show you which track of the CD goes with which section of the book.

Everything You Need to Know

I'll start by teaching you how to hold the harmonica, and how to make great sounds by breathing through it.

After that, I'll describe an incredibly simple system of reading harmonica music, and you'll be ready to go on to Blues, Rock, Folk, and even a bit of country music!

For your convenience, I'll put all the most important information in **boxes** — like this one.

In a hurry? Just read from box to box, and try every single "**Practice Session**" — they're marked with little music notes.

And play each of the songs and exercises, when you get to them.

Look at That "Mississippi Saxophone!"

Your harmonica should have ten little holes. Take a look at 'em. If you're *really new* to harmonica playing, remember this: you'll be breathing in and out of the side with the ten little holes!

How to Hold Your Harmonica

Right now, it's really not important how you hold the harmonica (as long as your mouth can reach the little holes).

Later on, I'll teach you how to use the great tone technique known as the "**hand wah wah.**" But for now...

Use either hand to hold your harmonica (in the long run, the left hand is better, if it's not too uncomfortable).

Hold your harmonica just like you would hold a sandwich that you were going to eat — this is "**the sandwich grip!**"

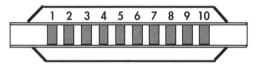

Make sure that you can see the **little numbers** on the top side of the harmonica.

Don't hold it **too tightly** — it's not heavy!

Just Use "The Sandwich Mouth" At First

The first harmonica instruction book that I tried to use really confused me. It said to cover four holes with my mouth, then block three of them with my tongue. I tried to do that a few times — with no success — then quit in disgust.

I later found out that this "tongue blocking" was an old-fashioned way of playing single holes. It's good to know about, but **not** for beginners!

The sound you get from playing any three holes at once is called a "**chord**" (pronounced "cord"). The sound you get from playing any one hole at a time (which you'll want to learn, eventually) is called a "**note**."

Luckily for beginners, there is no reason to worry about getting one single hole at a time yet! The harmonica is made so that we can play a few holes at a time, and it still sounds just fine!

So put the harmonica in your mouth — **just like a sandwich,** again — with your lips **covering about three holes.** That's a comfortable mouth size for most people.

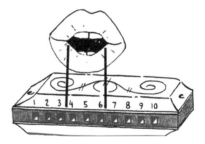

Breathing Practice ❷

Let's practice playing some different chords. We'll start in the middle part of the harmonica, then go to the high part and the low part.

Here are two important hints:

- Really try to notice when you are breathing **in**, and when you are breathing **out**! It makes a big difference!

- And try **not** to let any air go in or out **through your nose** while you are playing. Breathe through your mouth only!

Right Down the Middle

♪ With your mouth about "three holes wide," cover the holes that are in the **middle** of your harmonica.

These are the holes below the numbers **4, 5, and 6.**

Breathe in, and breathe out. Now you're playing two different chords — one on the in breath, and another on the out breathe.

Don't worry about exactly which holes you are covering. Just generally aim at the middle of the harmonica, for this exercise. The harmonica is very forgiving! If you are only "one hole off," it usually won't make too much difference, at first.

♪ Try Some High Notes

Keep your mouth about "three holes wide." Now breathe in and out through the **higher** holes. These are the holes below the higher numbers, like **8, 9, and 10.** Breathe softly up here, or you could get kinda shrill!

♪ Down So Low

Finally, breathe in and out through the **low** holes — the holes below the numbers **1, 2, and 3.**

A Little Warning: If you get a "choked" or "funky" sound down here when breathing in, don't worry, yet! Do make sure that your mouth is at least "three holes wide," and try to relax your tongue and throat while you play.

A Good Breathing Hint

If you know that you are going to start off with an "out" chord, make sure you start with your lungs filled! Starting on an "in" chord? Get empty, first!

Ready! Aim! Play!

Here's the good news and the bad news. The good news is that you don't have to worry about getting single holes yet. The "bad" news is that you do have to learn to find and **aim** your mouth at particular holes.

What does **"aim your mouth at a particular hole"** mean? For example, I might want you to play hole #5. I don't mind if hole #4 and hole #6 creep in along with hole #5. But I do want you to be **aimed** at hole #5 — that is, the middle of your mouth should be centered on hole #5.

"Aim at the number, but don't worry about the neighbors!"

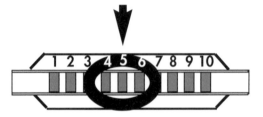

Writing Harmonica Music

There are a number of different ways to write music down. Most classical musicians use what is called **"standard notation,"** which has lots of note symbols placed on lines. Standard notation takes most people a long time to learn. So I don't use it for my harmonica books.

Instead, I use what is called **"tablature"** to write harmonica music.

Tablature tells you **which holes** to cover with your mouth, and whether to breathe **in** or **out.** It's super easy!

David's Harmonica Notation

The **numbers** tell you which hole to aim your mouth at. If I want you to aim your mouth at **holes 4, 5, and 6,** I write:

<u>456</u>
↑

The underlining reminds you to play all three holes at one time.

Now I have to tell you whether to **breathe in, or breathe out.**

Outlined style numbers mean breathe **out!**

So 456 means breathe <u>OUT</u> on holes <u>4</u>, <u>5</u>, and <u>6</u>

Filled in style numbers mean breathe **in!**

So **234** means breathe <u>IN</u> on holes <u>2</u>, <u>3</u>, and <u>4</u>

Jingle Bells (Take One!)

Now I have an easy way to tell you what holes to aim at, and whether to breathe in or out on them.

The only other thing you need to know is **how long** to make each sound. This is easy, if you know what a song sounds like.

Let's try playing **_Jingle Bells._** To play the first line of **_Jingle Bells_**, aim your lips at hole #5, and cover holes #4 and #6 also. Start with a lungful of air, and whisper the words of the song (don't say them out loud) through the harmonica.

• If you know what the song **_Jingle Bells_** sounds like, try this Practice Session right now. If you don't, keep on reading.

♪ _Jingle Bells_

jin	gle	bells	(quick breathe)	jin	gle	bells
456	456	456		456	456	456

The Fine Art of Articulation

Whispering the words of a song through our harmonica "breaks up" the sound into pieces, in the right places. To get a sharper or clearer sound, us harmonica players also whisper "**articulations**" through our harmonicas. These are just words that sound clearer than regular words, like "**doo**" or "**too**" or "**tah.**"

Replace the whispered words "Jingle Bells" with some whispered "doo" articulations, like this:

♪ _Jingle Bells,_ **With Articulations**

doo	doo	dooooo	(quick breath)	doo	doo	dooooo
456	456	456		456	456	456

♪ Try whispering some "doo" or "too" or "tah" articulations through your harmonica, anywhere — low, middle, or high!

♪ ***Taps*** ❹

The first line of ***Taps*** is a bit harder than Jingle Bells, since **you need to move** from the 234 out chord to the 345 out chord. How far is that? Look at your harmonica to see! You'll figure it out, with a bit of practice.

If you don't know this great campfire song, the timing dots will help! Start with your lungs full, but catch a quick breath in between the "Day" and the "is," if you really need to. Try whispering the words, and then try articulating some "doos."

Day	is	done		doo	doo	dooooo
234	234	345	**or**	234	234	345

Sometimes I will write down songs by just telling you which hole to aim your mouth at. But I don't expect you to play just one hole!

Day	is	done		doo	doo	dooooo
3	3	4	**or**	3	3	4

Timing Dots

Of course, sometimes (especially for Blues and Rock players) you'll be learning songs that you don't already know. Or maybe you don't know what ***Jingle Bells*** or ***Taps*** sound like! So I include **"timing dots"** in my harmonica notation.

The Steady Beat

All music has a **"steady beat,"** just like a heartbeat or your pulse. When playing or listening to music, it's natural (and a good habit) to tap your foot once for each beat.

My **"timing dots"** • • • tell you exactly when you would tap your foot, when playing a song.

Practice tapping your foot in a steady "one two three four" beat. The time between each beat should be exactly the same.

Playing Songs from Notation

Try playing **Jingle Bells** and **Taps** again. This time, we'll use the timing dots. And there's more timing dot info on the next page. Can you tap your foot and play at the same time? It's a great skill to have!

Ready? Fill your lungs, and start by aiming your mouth at hole #5 for **Jingle Bells**, and hole #3 for **Taps**. Don't worry if the neighbors come in!

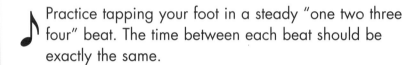

jin	gle	bells	(quick breathe)	jin	gle	bells	
•	•	•	•	•	•	•	out = breathe out
456	456	456		456	456	456	

Day	is	done	(quick	breathe)	Night's	be	gun
•		••		•	•		•••
234	234	345			234	345	456

Hint: Hum the song and tap your foot while you look at the dots!

Multiple Dots, No Dots, and Silent Dots

Some chords have one dot over them — no problem — play 'em for one beat. One dot, one foot tap, one beat. But some chords have two dots, or three, or none. Confused? Here's what they mean:

Two Dots or Three Dots: Hold the chord for two or three beats.

No Dot (like "is" in *Taps*): Chord plays while your foot is in between taps.

Dot without chord: The dot after the word "bells" is a **"silent beat,"** because it has no hole numbers under it. Tap your foot once before you start on the next "Jingle," and catch a breath during that tap!

Bluesy Train and ⑤ Breathing Patterns

Almost all of my beginning Blues and Rock songs will be based on "**breathing patterns**." Breathing patterns are just rhythms of in and out breaths that we memorize. I'll teach you two of my favorites, so you can play The Bluesy Train!

The Count of Four

Start this (and any other) exercise by tapping your foot four times. Doing that (called "a **count of four**") will help you to keep up a steady beat while you play the exercise. That's why I put the four dots before the chord notation in the following exercise.

A Train Whistle Breathing Pattern: Starting on an "In"

Cover the holes 4, 5, and 6 with your mouth. Start nice and **empty,** so you can give me two separate beats of **456 in** chord.

• • • •   •   •   •   •

"one two three four" **456** **456**   (silent beats)

Now try it two times in a row, like this:

Filled in = breathe in

•   •   •   •   •   •   •   •

456 **456** (silent) **456** **456** (silent)

"Doo" the Whistle

If you want to try articulation on an in chord, add a few "doo's" for a punchier whistle. Just start empty, keep your nose shut, and whisper "doo" on the inhale!

doo   doo   doo   doo
•   •   •   •   •   •   •

456   **456** (silent) **456**   **456** (silent)

Train Wheels Hints to Avoid "Funky" Sound:

Remember to keep your mouth wide, covering the 1, 2, and 3 holes completely. Your upper lip is on top of the harmonica, lower lip underneath, so that the harmonica is way in between your lips. Eat that "tin sandwich!"

Relax your throat and tongue as much as you can!

♪ The Train Wheels Breathing Pattern

Practice this breathing pattern without your harmonica but with a steady beat, while tapping your foot.

•   •   •   •   •   •   •   •

"one two three four"   **in**   **in**   out   out

Cover the holes 1, 2, and 3 with your mouth. Start nice and **empty,** since you will be starting off with two separate beats of

123 in chord. Then you'll play two separate beats of 123 out chord.

• • • •   •   •   •   •

"one two three four **123** **123** 123 123

in	= breathe in
out	= breathe out

Now try it two times in a row, like this:

• • • • • • • •

123 **123** 123 123 **123** **123** 123 123

Practice the Train Wheels Breathing Pattern until you can do it lots of times in a row, without getting too full of air or too empty.

If you find yourself getting too full, hit the out chords harder! Too empty? Draw in more air on the in chords!
A bit dizzy? Sit down and take a break. Your lungs will get used to playing, in a week or so!

 A Train of Your Own

Make up your own train by changing the **speed** of the Train Wheel Breathing Pattern. Learn to play it fast, for a train speeding through the countryside. Slow it down as it approaches the station. If it's leaving the station, start slowly, then build speed as the train gets going!

Train Wheels and Whistle

Combine the two train breathing patterns to make up more exciting train songs of your own. Here's a short one — make yours much longer!

♪ Beginning the Bluesy Train

Be ready to move your mouth from the 123 out chord to the **456 in** chord. After you play the **456 in** whistles, you have two silent beats to get back to the **123 in** part of the train wheels. That's plenty of time to move your mouth down, but make sure that your lungs are empty for those two **123 in** chords.

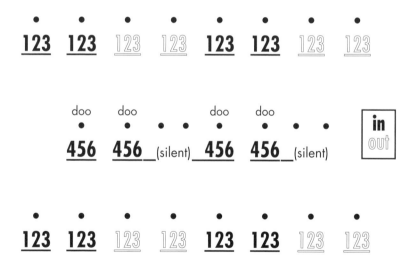

123 123 123 123 **123 123** 123 123

doo doo   doo doo

456 456 (silent) **456 456** (silent)   in/out

123 123 123 123 **123 123** 123 123

Harmonica Tone for Beginners

> **One simple habit** can really improve your harmonica tone, for the rest of your playing life! You don't need to study these hints right now, just come back to this section later on. But if your train wheels sound "choky" or "funky" to you, keep readin' and give these suggestions a try.

That habit is keeping your **air passage as open as possible**, from your diaphragm (breathing) muscle above your stomach, all the way up to your lips. So, from the top down...

Don't let your lips block your sound. No matter how many holes you are covering, keep your upper lip on top of the harmonica, and your lower lip under it.

Keep the inside of your mouth as open as possible while playing. This means that your tongue and throat must stay relaxed. Keeping your shoulders low and relaxed will also help.

Try to pull the breath in, and push it out, from your stomach. (Actually, your diaphragm muscle, just above your stomach.) This is an advanced technique, and covered in detail in my other books and CDs.

The Hand Shake or Head Shake

My favorite technique for adding exciting tone to the harmonica is the "**shake.**" It can be used anywhere on the harmonica, in or out, but you can start by adding it to your train whistle.

Just shake the harmonica from side to side about one quarter inch, while playing the **456 in** chord. Can you hear a "shimmery" tone?

I use a little shaky line wwwwwwwwwwwwwww under a chord to tell you when to shake that chord.

> It works best if you do not move the harmonica back and forth too far.

For a really neat whistle, shake with your hand and "doo" with your mouth at the same time, like this:

```
        doo     doo                  doo     doo
         •       •    •     •          •       •    •     •
♪      456     456  (silent)       456     456  (silent)
       wwww    wwww                 wwww    wwww
```

Realistic Trains

You can make your trains really realistic by thinking about what the train is doing, and where YOU are in relationship to the train. How's that?

Well, if you're **on the train,** the loudness always stays the same, but the speed changes, depending on what the train is doing.

If you're at the station, and the train is **coming towards you,** here's what you hear. First, a faint, faraway whistle. Then, a moment later, the first faint, fast, train wheel sounds, and a louder whistle. The wheels and whistle get louder and louder, and slower and slower, until the train reaches the station with a very loud last whistle!

If the train is **leaving,** the reverse is true. It starts slow and loud, and gets faster and softer, until the wheel sounds are gone and you can barely hear a final whistle in the distance.

A Bit of Review

Can you play the first lines of **Jingle Bells** (page 16) and **Taps** (page 17), and the **Train Wheel Breathing Pattern** (page 20), from my notation?

If not, you might want to go back to pages 13, 16, and 17 and review my notation system before going on...

Play the Harmonica—Today!

Now that you have the harmonica basics down, you're ready to go on to play your first Blues (page 25), Rock (page 36), or Folk (page 42) song — within the next few minutes!

After sampling each style, you'll be able to decide what you want to do with the rest of your harmonica-playing career! Perhaps, like me, you will discover that you love to play all styles of music. Because the more styles you can play in, the better you can express your own feelings and creativity!

A Hint to Rockers

Since Rock music is based on Blues music, you rock and rollers should probably do at least the first half of the Blues Section before starting the Rock section. You'll enjoy it more if you pay your dues to the Blues!

Play the Blues—Today ❼

There are many different styles of Blues music. They all came from the African musical tradition, where music was used both to express strong feelings, and to help people deal with those feelings. As I like to say in my corporate workshops: "One hundred years ago there was no Prozac. Freud was an unknown. But people had the Blues, and they got rid of them by playing them!"

From here on, you don't have to read all the words, but you will need to **play all the music** written in notation — no more music notes!

Playing Solo, Playing with Others

It's fun to play harmonica solo — that is, all by ourselves, walkin' down the road. But it may be even more fun to play Blues along with other musicians. If you have the **CD** for this method, you'll have lots of **Blues Band background music** that I've recorded to play along with.

The Chicago Blues "Riff"

We'll start with a Chicago style Blues "**Riff**." A riff is a short phrase or chunk of music that we memorize, then play again, usually along with other musicians.

So put your lips over the <u>456</u> chord, and get really **empty** — there's a long in coming! Make the single out breath sharp and forceful, then pull the in breath back with vigor! Afterwards, you have **three silent beats** to recover in, before you do it again!

```
•  •  •  •        •••    •      •    •••
```

"one two three four"   **456** 456 **456**_(silent)

Two "Bars," Chicago Style

This riff is called a "**Two Bar Riff.**" A "**bar**" is a Blues and Rock music term that usually means "**four beats.**" Since our Chicago Riff is eight beats long (count 'em if you don't believe me), it is also two bars long.

Shakin' The Chicago Blues Riff

Let's try playing two Chicago Blues Riffs in a row. Make sure that you get empty by the end of the three silent beats. And add some shake to your riff. You can just shake the long in chord (first line). Or you can shake the whole riff (second line) by shaking steadily while you change from in to out to in.

```
•  •  •  •        •••    •      •    •••
```

"one two three four" **456** 456 **456**_(silent)
                     wwww

| **in** = breathe in |
| **out** = breathe out |

```
                   •••    •      •    •••
```

456 456 **456**_(silent)
wwwwwwwwwwwwwwwwww

Third Position Chicago Blues

This riff is in "**Third Position**." "**Positions**" tell us what "**key**" harmonica to use when — it's a form of music theory. I've got a book on it, natch!

The Twelve Bar Blues ❽

"**The Twelve Bar Blues**" is just a musical term for the most popular form of Blues. Anyone who likes Blues music has heard of them (although some of us didn't used to know what the term meant).

In the Twelve Bar Blues, each verse of the Blues song is exactly Twelve Bars — or **48 beats** — long. (Why 48 beats? Since one bar = four beats, and 4 beats x 12 bars = 48 beats.)

Your Chicago Twelve Bar Blues

Our Chicago Riff is only eight beats (or two bars) long. So we will have to play it **six times** to make up one Twelve Bar Blues Verse. (8 beats x 6 = 48, or 2 bars x 6 = 12 bars)

Each verse of a Twelve Bar Blues is usually made up of three different chords. So we'll have to use **three different versions** of our Chicago Riff. We'll do one version in the middle of the harmonica (just like we've been doing). We'll also learn two new ones — one up a little higher, and one way up high.

The new versions of the Chicago Blues Riff (for the Chicago Twelve Bar Blues) are easy to do. Just put your mouth over a different chord, and use the same **exact breathing pattern.**

Don't worry about exactly which holes you're on — just aim at the middle for the "main" riff (the one you've already practiced). Start out with four foot taps, then play two in the middle.

Go up a little higher for the third one, and back to the middle for the fourth riff. Go way up high for the fifth one, then finish off with one back in the middle. Add some shake whenever you like. **Sounds like the Blues!**

And **start listening** for that Twelve Bar Blues structure. Soon you'll be able to hear how each verse of a Blues repeats this fascinating structure.

Your First Chicago Twelve Bar Blues

If you'd like to, learn the **names** for each part of a Twelve Bar Blues, at left.

	• • •	•	•	• • •	• • •	•	•	• • •
("Tonic" or I Chord)	**456**	456	**456**	(silent)	**456**	456	**456**	(silent)

	• • •	•	•	• • •
("Subdominant" or IV Chord)	**678**	678	**678**	(silent)

in
out

28

("Second Tonic" ••• • • •••
or Second
I Chord) **456** 456 **456**__(silent)

••• • • •••
("Dominant" **8910** 8910 **8910** (silent)
or V Chord)

("Third Tonic" ••• • • •••
or Third
I Chord) **456** 456 **456**__(silent)   This verse ends.

The Boogie Woogie
Twelve Bar Blues ❾

By learning a new breathing pattern, we'll be able to play the toe-tappin' New Orleans style "**Boogie Woogie Twelve Bar Blues!**" This is best done along with background music.

The Boogie Woogie Breathing Pattern

Make the changes from in to out to in forcefully — Move that air, right down from your stomach! Notice that the **last two chords share a single beat "out/in!"** — the in gets pulled back in right after the out, then there are two silent beats (although it may be hard to hear the first one, even with the CD). Try it a few times without your harmonica.

• • • • • • • •
in out **in** out **in** out **in** (silent beats)

> Spending a few minutes now with the Folk section (page 42) may improve your "**aiming**" and "**puckering**" skills for the Boogie Woogie!!

The <u>45</u> Boogie Woogie

Pucker your lips down to just two holes wide. Then put them over the <u>45</u> holes, and give me a Boogie Woogie Breathing Pattern. Keep it crisp and forceful!

| **45** | 45 | **45** | 45 | **45** | 45 | **45** | | **in**
out |

(silent beats)

Your First Boogie Woogie Twelve Bar Blues

Just like we did with the Chicago Riff, we'll learn two new versions, one a bit higher, and one way up high. Then we'll make a Twelve Bar Blues out of the Boogie Woogie Breathing Pattern.

> Once again, **don't worry** about exactly which holes you are on. Pucker up a little (two holes wide), and play the breathing pattern **in the middle** (<u>45</u>), **a little higher** (around <u>56</u> or <u>67</u>), and **way up high** (<u>89</u> or <u>9 10</u>).

The Walkin' Boogie Woogie Blues

Once you've learned the Boogie Woogie Breathing Pattern, you can learn to move around **during** the pattern! For example, start out in the **middle** (around the 45, say) then as you breathe in and out work your way up to the **high end.** I don't really care exactly what notes you use. So think of it like this, rather than thinking about specific hole numbers.

middle start   end up way high

in   out   **in**   out   **in**   out   **in**

And, of course, you can do the reverse: Start way up high and in and out your way down to the middle. Or breathe your way from the low end up to the middle. Or from the middle down to the low end.

Shake That Boogie Woogie

Why not? Shake while you're walkin' a Boogie Woogie Breathing Pattern. It sounds great!

Using Just a Few Holes

Try some that just use a few holes, like <u>34</u> and <u>45</u>, or <u>34</u>, <u>45</u> and <u>56</u>. Listen to my examples on the CD, and hear how I fit six of these into a Twelve Bar Blues. Here's a favorite that uses three holes.

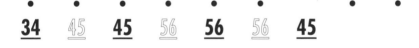

Once you've got the Boogie Woogie Breathing Pattern, walk it around **while** you breathe in and out. Take it low to middle, middle to high, high to middle, low to high, whatever!

Shake it and "dwah" it, as you walk it! Keep up the breathing pattern, and don't think too much! Make up your own versions!

If you've got the CD, just jam along with the Boogie Woogie Twelve Bar Blues, and listen to my examples and verbal instructions. You can't go wrong with this one!

Bending and "Dwah-ing" the Boogie Woogie Blues ⑩

If you've already practiced articulating on the in breath (page 19, "Doo" the Train Whistle), you can learn a great tone effect. All Blues harmonica players **have to** learn to "**bend**" notes — that growling, crying sound that we love so much.

You can get a "pre-bending" effect by whispering the word "**dwah**" through the harmonica on an in breath. Start empty, keep your lips puckered down to two holes, and exaggerate the whispered "dwah." Can you hear the sound change? Now "dwah" each in breath of your Boogie Woogie Breathing Pattern!

Don't forget the extra playalong music at the end of the CD!

The Bluesified Train ⑪

For a wonderful solo playing experience, turn your train into a Blues. Here's how to do it!

Step One: The Chugga Train

Whisper the word "**chugga**" through your harmonica, on every out breath of the train, like this:

in = breathe in
out = breathe out

Step Two: Riff Whistles for the Blues Train

When you can play the "chugga" train smoothly, substitute a **Chicago Riff** or a **Boogie Woogie Riff** for the whistle. Here's a very short example below, but make up much longer ones of your own.

   •   •   chugga   chugga   •   •   chugga   chugga
                •   •   •   •

123   **123**   123   123   **123**   **123**   123   123

Chicago Riff   •••   •   •   •••

456   456   **456**_ (silent)

wwwww

   •   •   chugga   chugga   •   •   chugga   chugga

123   **123**   123   123   **123**   **123**   123   123

Boogie Woogie Riff   dwah   dwah   dwah
           •   •   •   •   •   •   ••

45   45   **45**   45   **45**   45   **45**

   •   •   chugga   chugga   •   •   chugga   chugga

123   **123**   123   123   **123**   **123**   123   123

One of My Favorite Solo Blues Riffs ⑫

This fabulous riff is used in hundreds of Blues songs, by dozens of artists. In Rock songs, TV commercials, and movies, too. Start with this simplified version to get the breathing right. Tap your foot once for each beat. If you can, tap harder for the bigger beats — they're the "real" beats.

123 123 **123** **123**   (sing or silent)

When that feels comfortable, we'll only tap on the "real" beats.

123 123 **123** **123**   (sing or silent)

Now move the out breath to the 345 out chord, and hit a **34 in** (with a "dwah," if you can manage it) before ending up on that last **123 in**. It's well worth the effort — it's a classic!

The Real Solo Blues Rappin' Riff!

               dwah
123 345 **34** **123**   "a beat and a beat"

The Blues Scale

Perhaps you wonder why we use the notes we use in these riffs and Twelve Bars. All Blues Riffs, Solos, and Songs are based on a "**musical alphabet of the Blues**" called "**The Blues Scale.**"

Once you understand The Blues Scale, and begin to "bend" notes, you can create a lifetime of your own Blues Music, and play anyone else's... Here's what the easiest "Second Position" or **"Cross Position" Blues Scale** looks like — but you'll need to learn lots more about it soon!

2	**3**	4	**4**	**4**	**5**	6	**in** out
	bend		bend				

Where to Go From Here

If you have enjoyed playing these most basic Blues so far, you might want to check out some of my other material.

Instant Blues Harmonica (book & CD) will help you to learn to create your own improvised Blues, based on the Blues Scale.

Three Minutes to™ Blues Harmonica (video) is the absolute easiest way to learn the Blues, with my amazing Harmonica Hand Signal™ Method. ***Blues and Rock Harmonica Made Easy*** (book) can be used as a workbook with the video, or by itself to learn lots of great riffs and solos.

Bending the Blues (book & CD) is a must for anyone who wants to keep playin' the Blues. It goes from total beginner level ("What *is* a Bend?") to advanced bending techniques like "blow or overblow bends."

Blues and Rock Harp Positions Made Easy is a complete music theory book for harp players (no reading music necessary). If you want to play with other musicians, this one will help you — a lot!

Play Rock and Roll—Today! ⑬

Rock is the child of the Blues. One main difference between the two styles of music is in the beat. When playing Blues, we usually emphasize the first beat of every bar (four beat chunk). In rock, we emphasize the second and fourth beats. This rhythm's called the "**Rock Backbeat**."

Blues Beat: 1   2   3   4
Rock Beat: 1   **2**   3   **4**

The Two Bar Rock Bridge

Put your lips on the <u>45</u> chord, and start **very empty!** Hit the out chord sharply and forcefully (you'll probably need to)! Throw some shake on the in chord, and articulate some "dwahs" during it also, if you like.

●   ●   ●   ●   ●●●●   ●   ●●●

"one two three four"   **<u>45</u>**   <u>45</u>   (silent)
                         www

The Rock Breathing Pattern

This exciting two bar (eight beat) breathing pattern can be used anywhere on the harmonica, just like all our other breathing patterns. Make the changes from in to out chord sharp and percussive! Practice it without the harmonica for a minute. Start with four taps of your foot (not shown). Try this great breathing pattern on the <u>45</u> chord first, then on the <u>123</u> chord, to prepare for a hot Twelve Bar!

●   ●   ●   ●   ●   ●   ●   ●   ● ●

in   **in**   out   **in**   **in**   out   **in**   **in**   out   **in**

Twelve Bar Rock n' Roll!

Combine the Rock Bridge with the Rock Breathing Pattern to create a **Twelve Bar Rock & Roll Verse!** The three different "versions" fit into the six "parts" of the Twelve Bar, just like in Chicago and Boogie Woogie Twelve Bar Blues. (I've marked those "I, IV and V" Chord names for you.)

I   <u>123</u> <u>123</u> <u>123</u>   <u>123</u> <u>123</u> <u>123</u>   <u>123</u> <u>123</u> <u>123</u>   <u>123</u>

I   <u>123</u> <u>123</u> <u>123</u>   <u>123</u> <u>123</u> <u>123</u>   <u>123</u> <u>123</u> <u>123</u>   <u>123</u>

IV   <u>45</u> <u>45</u> <u>45</u>   <u>45</u> <u>45</u> <u>45</u>   <u>45</u> <u>45</u> <u>45</u>   <u>45</u>

I   <u>123</u> <u>123</u> <u>123</u>   <u>123</u> <u>123</u> <u>123</u>   <u>123</u> <u>123</u> <u>123</u>   <u>123</u>

V   <u>45</u>   <u>45</u>   (silent)
wwww

I   <u>123</u> <u>123</u> <u>123</u>   <u>123</u> <u>123</u> <u>123</u>   <u>123</u> <u>123</u> <u>123</u>   <u>123</u>

Walkin' the Rock Breathing Pattern

As with the Boogie Woogie Breathing Pattern, you will want to learn to "**walk around the harmonica**" while doing the Rock Breathing Pattern. Start anywhere, and end up anywhere else, while maintaining that in in out pattern. Listen to my Twelve Bar Rock Pattern Blues on the CD, then make up some of your own!

Whole Lotta Shakin' and Jumpin' and "Dwah"in'

Add some shakes during the Rock Breathing Pattern. Don't be afraid to jump around on it, either. Do some in chords down low, on 123, but jump to some out chords on 456, for example. Try whispering "**dwahdas**" on all the 123 in beats, sometimes, for a funkier sound!

dwah   da   dwah   da   dwah   da
•   •   •   •   •   •   •   • •
123 123 456 **123 123** 123 **123 123** 456 **456**

wwwwwwwwwwwwwwwwwwwwwwwwwwwwwwwwwwwww

The Rock Boogie ⓮

The "**Rock Boogie**" is a simple but satisfying type of rock that can be played solo or with other musicians (or the CD). Remember to **emphasize** (play louder) the **second and fourth beats** of each bar. Here's the simplest version.

            louder   louder
•   •   •   •
123   123   234   345

Break the second beat into two parts, for a more interesting Boogie. It may be easier to do this by inhaling a few "da's" (short articulations) instead of using separate puffs of air. In fact, why not try "doo-ing" all the in chords, for a punchier sound. "Dwah" the **234 in**, if you can!

doo **da!** da dwah **da!**
• • • •
123 **123** **123** **234** 345

For the best Boogie, cut the 345 out chord off sharply (half a beat's worth). Then **slide** down on the **in breath**, just in time to start the next **123 in** chord. You'll need to **get empty** on that short 345 out!

doo da da dwah (shortened)
• • • •
123 **123** **123** **234** 345   in slide down

doo da da dwah (shortened)
• • • •
123 **123** **123** **234** 345   in slide down

The Bluesy Boogie

Just as you did with the train, add Chicago or Boogie Woogie style riffs to your Boogie. Just play the Boogie for a while, then throw in one of the other Two Bar riffs, then come back to the Boogie. It sounds great, and you can create a million variations by inserting different riffs. Listen to my recorded examples, then do it with me for an hour or so!

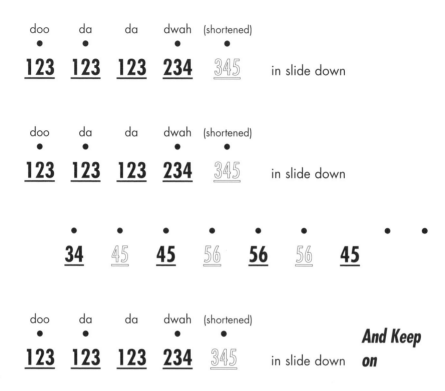

doo   da   da   dwah (shortened)
•   •   •   •   •
123 **123** **123** **234** 345   in slide down

doo   da   da   dwah (shortened)
•   •   •   •   •
123 **123** **123** **234** 345   in slide down

•   •   •   •   •   •   •   •
34 45 **45** 56 **56** 56 **45**

doo   da   da   dwah (shortened)
•   •   •   •
123 **123** **123** **234** 345   in slide down ***And Keep on***

The 1950's Rock and Roll Ballad ⓯

This **"Four Bar Rock Ballad"** style verse was used in lots of 1950's and early 1960's style Rock, including many old favorites like ***Duke of Earl*** or ***Earth Angel***.

Here are two verses. The first is very simple, but try to squeeze down your lips a bit to get closer to one hole at a time. (Keep the upper lip on top, and the lower lip on the bottom, natch.)

I'll write these down as though you were playing single holes. Just do the best you can, and use two hole chords if you need to, right now. (Or go to the Folk section on page 42, and practice!) Start with lungs empty, and with a count of four foot taps, to get your timing ready (not shown). Be prepared to catch a good breath between the long 2 out and long 1 out. Here's the first verse:

2　　　2　　　1　　　**1**

And here's the second verse. After you've practiced both, play the first verse once, then the second verse, then the first verse again, fading it out at that last 1 in. This makes a sweet sounding three verse Rock Ballad. Use hand wah wahs anywhere you like.

• • • •　　• • • •
2 3 4 5　　2 3 **3 4**

• • • •　• • • •
1 2 3 2　**1**

Where to Go For More Rock

If you've enjoyed this rock section, you'll find more in **Instant Blues Harmonica, Three Minutes to™ Blues Harmonica,** and **Blues and Rock Harmonica Made Easy.** And **Instant Blues Harmonica Volume Two** features lots of great Rock riffs and solos. If you can play all the rock in this book, you might even be ready to go straight to IBH Vol. Two now, if you really like to rock and are willing to work on Bending!

Play Folk Music—Today! 🔟

What campfire would be complete without a harmonica folk song? None — so let's start right now by learning the distance between some of the out chords. Look at your harmonica for a moment, to study the distance between holes.

With your mouth nice and wide, aim at hole #3. Your lungs should be full. Play these four chords. If you need to, catch a quick breath in between each chord.

• • • •   •   •   •   •

"one two three four"   234   345   456   567

| **in** = breathe in |
| **out** = breathe out |

Taps 🔟

If you can play the above chords, you're ready for Taps! Unlike most songs, it only uses out notes. Play it slowly, and add shakes or hand wah wahs (page 43) on the long notes.

To make the notation easier to read, I will only tell you which hole to aim at, not the entire chord. But keep your mouth wide as you like. Remember — dots show you when your foot should tap. And fill 'er up — it's all on out notes!

•   ••   •   •   ••   •

3   3   4   3   4   5

$$\bullet \quad\quad \bullet \quad \bullet \quad\quad \bullet \quad \bullet \quad\quad \bullet\bullet \quad \bullet$$
3 4 5   3 4 5   3 4 5

$$\bullet \quad\quad \bullet\bullet \quad \bullet \quad \bullet \quad\quad \bullet\bullet \quad \bullet \quad \bullet \quad\quad \bullet\bullet\bullet$$
4 5 6   5 4 3   3 3 4

The Hand Wah Wah

If you plan to play one-handed (while you cook, fish, or commute), then it's never going to matter how you hold it. But for a "hand wah wah," hold the harmonica in your left hand as pictured above.

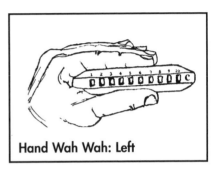

Hand Wah Wah: Left

Then use your right hand to open and close the space in front of your harmonica. Everyone has different shaped hands, so experiment to find the hand arrangement that suits you!

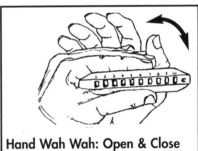

Hand Wah Wah: Open & Close

Puckering Down Your Lips

See if you can cover two — or even one — holes with your lips, instead of three. Just pucker your lips down a bit, as though you were getting ready to kiss someone!

Make sure that as you pucker, your lips do not block the air flow. Your upper lip should still be on top of the harmonica, and your lower lip under it. You're only tightening the sides of your mouth in a little. Aim the center of your pucker right into the hole that you are trying to get.

"Musical Alphabets" ⓲

Blues music is based on the "**musical alphabet**" known as the "**Blues Scale**." Most Country music is based on the musical alphabet called the "**Country Pentatonic Scale**." And most Folk music is based on the musical alphabet known as the "**Major Scale**."

DO	RE	ME	FA	SO	LA	TI	DO
4	**4**	5	**5**	6	**6**	**7**	7

in = breathe in
out = breathe out

The Major Scale

We'll begin by learning to play the first six notes of the Major Scale. Many great Folk songs use just these six notes. Don't worry about single noting until you can play it easily with chords, like this.

DO	RE	ME	FA	SO	LA	
345	**345**	456	**456**	567	**567**	or (one hole)
4	**4**	5	**5**	6	**6**	

Preparing for Twinkle Twinkle Little Star

Take a minute, and practice **jumping** from 345 out to 567 out. (If you are practicing single holes, jump from 4 out to 6 out.) Memorize that distance with your hand, then try this old favorite. Play it as wide as you like.

44

Twinkle Twinkle Little Star ⓳

Twin	kle	twin	kle	lit	tle	star		how	I	won	der	what	you	are
•	•	•	•	•	•	•	•	•	•	•	•	•	•	•
4	4	6	6	**6**	**6**	6		**5**	**5**	5	5	**4**	**4**	4

Up	a	bove	the	world	so	high		Like	a	dia	mond	in	the	sky
•	•	•	•	•	•	•	•	•	•	•	•	•	•	•
6	6	**5**	**5**	5	5	**4**		6	6	**5**	**5**	5	5	**4**

Twin	kle	twin	kle	lit	tle	star		how	I	won	der	what	you	are
•	•	•	•	•	•	•	•	•	•	•	•	•	•	•
4	4	6	6	**6**	**6**	6		**5**	**5**	5	5	**4**	**4**	4

Warning: Don't be hard on yourself if you can't play the song right the first time. This is supposed to be fun, not an opportunity for self-criticism! Try to learn half a line at a time, until you have the whole thing!

Playing By Ear: A Few Important Hints ⓴

It's fun, and not too hard, to figure out Folk songs by yourself (especially if I tell you the first few notes). Here are two important hints:

1) Practice the **first six notes of the Major Scale** — a lot.

DO	RE	ME	FA	SO	LA
345	**345**	456	**456**	567	**567**

2) Learn **a few Folk songs well** — like Taps, Twinkle Twinkle Little Star, and Oh When the Saints.

Oh When the Saints

Oh	when	the	saints		Go	mar	chin'	in		Oh	when	the	saints
•	•	•	••• ••		•	•	•	•• •••		•	•	•	••
4	5	**5**	6		4	5	**5**	6		4	5	**5**	6

go	mar	chin'	in		Lord	I	want		to	be	in	that	num	ber
••	••	••	•••• ••		•	•	••		•	•	••	•	•	• ••••• •
5	4	5	**4**		5	**4**	4		4	5	6	6	6	**5**

When	the	saints	go	mar	chin'	in
•	•	••	••	••	•• ••• ••	
5	**5**	6	5	4	**4**	4

First Lines of Some Great Songs

Figure out the rest of the song yourself, using holes 4, 5, and 6.

Mi	chael	row	the	boat	a	shore		Ha	le	lieu	yah
•	•	••		•	•	•	•	•	•	••••	•
4	5	6	5	6	**6**	6		5	6	**6**	6

Well	I	went	to	Al	a	ba	ma	with	a	ban	jo	on	my	knee
•		•	•	••		•	•	••		•		•		•••
4	**4**	5	6	6	**6**	6	5	4	**4**	5	5	**4**	4	**4**

Beethoven's 9th Symphony, Fourth Movement: The Ode to Joy

••	•	•	•	•	•	•	•	•	•	•	•	••		••	
5	**5**	6	6	**5**	5	**4**	4	4	**4**	5	5	**4**	4		

•	•	•	•	•	•	•	•	•	•	•	•	••		••
5	5	**5**	6	6	**5**	5	**4**	4	4	**4**	5	**4**	4	4

Jin	gle	bells		Jin	gle	bells		Jin	gle	all	the	way
•	•	•		•	•	•		•	•	•	•	•••
5	5	5		5	5	5		5	6	4	**4**	5

My Harmonica is Missing Notes! XX%#!

It sure is! Two Major Scale notes (FA & LA) are missing from the low end of your harmonica. When you just can't seem to find a note, jump up and try **6 in** — that's probably it. Try playing **Amazing Grace** (or **Silent Night** — start on 6 out) without jumping to a 6 in, and you'll understand!

A	maz	ing	Grace	how	sweet	the	sound		to	save	a	wretch	like	me
•	••	•	••	•	••	•	•		•	••	•	••	• •••	••
3	4	5	5	**4**	4	**6**	6		3	4	5	5	**4**	6

Si	i	lent	night	Ho	o	ly	night		all	is	calm		all	is	right
••		•	••	•		••	•		• ••	•	••		• ••	•	•••
6	**6**	6	5	6	**6**	6	5		**4**	**4**	**3**		4	4	3

A Word About Country & Western ㉑

If you like Country music, check out the "**Country Pentatonic Scale.**" It's the "musical alphabet" for the harp riffs found in most C & W songs. Play it (using single notes if you can) along with my country backing on the CD. Here it is, going up then down, just like I do on the recording.

•	•	•	•	•	•	•	•
1	2	**2**	**3**	**4**	5	6	

		•	•	•	•	•	•
		6	5	**4**	**3**	**2**	2	**1**

If you like this style of playing, check out my **Country and Western Harmonica Made Easy** book and cassette. It's got hundreds of licks, some way easier than this scale, and some way harder!

The Playalong Tracks   26

Here's a variety of good music, in stereo, to play along with: **Guitar Blues**, a **Rockin' Rock Band**, a **Sweet Background for Twinkle Twinkle Little Star**, some **Hard Rock Twelve Bars**, and a **'50's Rock Ballad**.

How to Keep on Learning Harmonica! Free Brochure!

I don't mean to give you a "hard sell." But if you've enjoyed the harmonica styles in this "Beginner's Sampler," I hope that you'll keep on learning! Here are some of the harp methods that I discussed earlier, in the book and on the CD. Or contact me for a free, detailed, brochure.

Instant Blues Harmonica: Book & CD. No harder than this book, but aimed at helping you to improvise and develop your own Blues/Rock style.

Three Minutes to Blues Harp: 70 minute video. Unbelievably easy way to get lots of new riffs with my amazing "Harmonica Hand Signal Method™."

Blues & Rock Harp Made Easy: Book. Lots of riffs and solos in the styles of great Blues and Rock players. Use it by itself or as a workbook with the video.

The Pocket Harmonica Songbook: 40 great folk songs, in my notation.

Bending the Blues: Book and CD. Easiest way to learn how to bend!

David's Jamming CD: 70 minutes of blues & rock to play along with!

Visit us online at
www.davidharp.com or **www.bluesharp.com**
